CINDY TAYLOR

Route 66 Unplugged

Trivia, Fun, Food and History in a Condensed Journey

Contents

Preface

Route 66: Embracing the Spirit

Welcome to "Route 66 Unplugged: Trivia, History, and Highlights," a journey into the heart of one of America's most iconic highways. Route 66, often fondly referred to as the Mother Road, is more than just a stretch of pavement connecting Chicago to Los Angeles. It's a symbol of freedom, adventure, and the endless possibilities of the open road. This book aims to peel back the layers of time and asphalt to uncover the rich heritage of stories, landmarks, and cultures that thrive along this legendary route.

During my extensive journeys along the storied expanse of Route 66, stretching from the bustling streets of Chicago to the sun-kissed shores of Santa Monica, I have cultivated a deep and abiding passion for the open road. This historic path has ingrained in me an understanding of the profound yearning it instills in the hearts and minds of those who traverse it, seeking to recapture its bygone era of glory. The route, with its eclectic mix of quaint diners, neon-lit motels, and timeless landscapes, symbolizes an era of simplicity and unbridled freedom, a nostalgic reminder of a more straightforward and unhurried time in American history.

In the following pages, we won't just revisit the well-trodden path of Route 66's history; we aim to delve into what this road has meant to America through its history, motels, neon signs, and stories. I will admit to a bias to the west side. Having traveled the entire road from Chicago to LA, I am partial to the portion that takes us across the desert.

We will explore those areas more, but make no mistake the entire road has shaped our country and our hearts. I have by no means explored all of the nooks and corners that still echo the past with tales that yearn to be heard.

"Unplugged" in our title is a commitment to exploration. It's an invitation to experience Route 66 not just as tourists, but as travelers eager to understand the soul of the road. It's about unplugging from our preconceptions and immersing ourselves in the stories, the scenery, and the spirit that makes Route 66 unique.

Welcome to Route 66, unplugged.

1

Chapter 1

The Birth of the Mother Road

In the early 20th century, America's burgeoning love affair with the automobile set the stage for a transformation in how people traveled and experienced their vast country. Amidst this backdrop, Route 66 was born. Officially established on November 11, 1926, Route 66 would not only change the landscape of America but also become a lasting symbol of freedom and adventure.

Unlike the linear, direct highways of today with their singular goal, of getting where you are going with great haste, Route 66 was a winding, 2,448-mile-long road that crossed eight states and three time zones. Its path, from the industrial hub of Chicago through the heartland's farm fields, across the Great Plains, over the Rocky Mountains, and finally to the Pacific Coast in California, encapsulated a cross-section of the American experience. This route was one of the first to be fully paved, a feat completed in 1938, and it quickly became the main artery of cross-country travel in the United States. It was a chance for us to connect with each other in a way that we were never able to do before.

In a matter of days, we could embark on a cross-country adventure in our cars, an option far more accessible than the costly alternatives of train or plane travel. This was a game-changer for the family unit. This opened doors for mobility that the "every man" had not known in the past. This was freedom. The Sunday drive took on a whole new meaning. A weekend getaway was now a week-long vacation. Hotels and motels began to pop up along highways as did gas stations and quick eateries. The open road, the wind in your hair, life was a highway…and the spirit of Route 66 was born.

The Mother Road, as Route 66 was affectionately known, was more than a highway; it was a lifeline during the Great Depression. In the 1930s, it served as a pathway for migration, particularly for those escaping the Dust Bowl, and seeking a better life in the West. John Steinbeck famously dubbed it "the Mother Road, the road of flight" in his novel "The Grapes of Wrath," capturing its essence as a route of hope and despair.

As the decades passed, Route 66 evolved with the nation. During World War II, it was a critical transport route for military supplies, leading to significant upgrades and changes. In the post-war era, as car ownership boomed, Route 66 became synonymous with the American road trip. Families packed into their cars to explore, teenagers sought the freedom of the open road, and travelers from all walks of life experienced the diverse cultures and landscapes of America.

Along its winding path, Route 66 was dotted with unique attractions and quirky landmarks that became integral to its character. From the towering Meramec Caverns billboards to the Blue Whale of Catoosa, these roadside attractions were more than mere stops; they were chapters in the story of Route 66, each with its own history and lore.

The creation of Route 66 marked a significant chapter in American history. It represented technological progress, a shifting cultural landscape, and the unyielding spirit of exploration that is still with

CHAPTER 1

us 85 years later

2

Chapter 2

Architectural Marvels and Roadside Attractions

As travelers embark on the journey along Route 66, they are greeted by an array of architectural wonders and roadside attractions, each with its own story that captures the essence of America's eclectic and spirited character. Route 66 showcases a rich tapestry of architectural styles. From Art Deco buildings in Tulsa to the Spanish Revival structures in Santa Fe, the road is a living museum of 20th-century American architecture. These buildings not only serve as waypoints on the journey but also as gateways to the various cultural influences that have shaped the region's Route 66 traverses.

The Mother Road's roadside attractions were born out of the need to capture the attention of travelers. These attractions range from the whimsical to the bizarre, each telling a story about the local culture and history. Any album claiming to have been down Route 66 must include some of these fundamental landmarks

Paul Bunyan

The towering figures of Paul Bunyan and the Muffler Men, are symbols of American folklore and kitsch.

The Blue Whale

The Blue Whale of Catoosa, OK a beloved family picnic spot and an icon of Route 66. Built in the 1970s as a swimming hole, now it is a favorite photo stop and picnic place. Swimming is restricted, but you can still walk through the iconic whale and visit the gift shop.

Cadillac Ranch

Cadillac Ranch in Amarillo, Texas, is a striking art installation that invites visitors to leave their mark on a lineup of half-buried vintage Cadillacs. Is it a work of art, is it a political statement, is it a joke? No one really knows. What we do know is that it has been a staple of the Route 66 scene since 1974 and was said to have been placed there by an infamous local artist. People stop there and leave their mark with spray paint. Now another local artist (to be discussed in a later section) is making his mark by collecting paint chips from these cars and creating a new "stone" and beautiful jewelry.

Tower Station

Tower Station and U-Drop Inn Cafe in Shamrock, TX boast to be one of the most well-known stops along Route 66. It still looks much like it did in its glory days and it received a nod in Pixar's movie "Cars".

No exploration of Route 66 would be complete without mentioning the classic diners and motels that line its route. These establishments, like the Cozy Dog Drive-In in Springfield, Illinois, home of the original hot dog on a stick, or the Wigwam Motels with their unique tepee-shaped rooms, offer more than just food and lodging; they provide a sense of nostalgia and a connection to a bygone era.

Tepee Curios Sign

Remember Route 66 is about exiting the highway. It's about the journey, the stops in towns like Tucumcuri, NM to see Tepee Curios, and to stay in the Blue Swallow Motel. This is a sweet stop to lose your way as you meander the road. You will feel like you have taken a step back into the past when front doors weren't locked, soda pop was a quarter and movies were a dime.

Many of these structures and attractions have faced challenges over the years, from the decline in Route 66 travel due to the Interstate Highway System to the ravages of time. Preservation efforts by local communities and Route 66 enthusiasts have been crucial in maintaining these landmarks. These efforts ensure that the architectural and cultural heritage of Route 66 continues to be celebrated and experienced by new generations.

Blue Swallow

3

Chapter 3

The Cultural Tapestry

Route 66 has long been more than a highway; it's a symbol of freedom and discovery that has captured the imagination of artists, musicians, and writers. Let's explore the profound influence of the Mother Road on American culture, weaving through the realms of music, literature, and cinema to showcase its enduring legacy.

Flo's Cafe from Pixar's "Cars"

Music has always been a key part of the Route 66 experience. The road has inspired countless songs that evoke the spirit of travel and adventure.

Perhaps the most famous is Bobby Troup's "Route 66," covered by artists like Nat King Cole and Chuck Berry, which invites listeners on a rollicking journey from Chicago to LA. The highway's eclectic mix of jazz, blues, rock, and country music reflects the diverse communities along its path and has played a significant role in the development of American popular music.

No self-respecting Route 66 enthusiast would dare be without their Route 66 playlist. The songs may vary, but we will all likely have some of the same fundamental driving songs that capture the heart of Route 66. Here are my top 25 songs that always begin my journey with:

My Ultimate Route 66 Playlist

1. Route 66 - Nat King Cole
2. Chicago - Count Basie and Tonie Bennett
3. Running on Empty - Jackson Brown
4. Listen to the Music - The Doobie Brothers
5. Take it Easy - Eagles
6. Walking Man - James Taylor
7. Hit the Road - Ray Charles
8. American Girl - Tom Petty & The Heartbreakers
9. Dreams - Fleetwood Mac
10. Glory Days. - Bruce Springsteen
11. Don't Stop Believin' - Journey
12. Reelin' In The Years - Steely Dan
13. Summer of 69 - Bryan Adams
14. Drivin' My Life Away - Eddie Rabbitt
15. Ramblin Man - The Allman Brothers
16. Hold on Loosely - 38 Special

17. Life is a Highway - Rascal Flatts
18. Fever - Peggy Lee
19. Mack the Knife - Bobby Darin
20. Mr. Sandman - The Chordettes
21. Fallin - Connie Francis
22. Wake Up Little Susie - The Everly Brothers
23. Country Roads - John Denver
24. How High the Moon - Les Paul and Mary Ford
25. Sway - Dean Martin

Route 66 has also been a rich source of inspiration for literature. John Steinbeck's "The Grapes of Wrath" is a seminal work published in 1939 that immortalizes the road as a symbol of escape and hope during the Great Depression. More than just a backdrop, Route 66 in literature often becomes a character itself, representing a journey of transformation and discovery.

In cinema, Route 66 has been both a setting and a narrative driver. Classic films like "Easy Rider" starring Peter Fonda and Dennis Hopper and the female counterpart "Thelma & Louise" with Susan Sarandon and Geena Davis both use the road to symbolize a quest for freedom and self-discovery.

In 1940, John Steinbeck's "The Grapes of Wrath" was released in theaters. Americans were able to see the Joad family set out as the Dust Bowl devastated their lives and watch as these souls traversed the Steinbeck's, "Mother Road" in search of a better life". The film version of "The Grapes of Wrath" was nominated for an amazing 7 academy awards and it eventually became one of the best movies ever made.

Perhaps Disney Pixar's animated film "Cars" brought Route 66 did the greatest job of bringing Route 66 to life AND bringing it to a new generation. If you are not familiar with the story, it is truly amazing.

In order to get the group of animators to truly grasp the lifestyle of the open road and freedom that is Route 66, they needed to experience it. They needed to ramble down the road and take the time to exit right and explore, instead of speeding by towns and landmarks. What better way to learn this than a road trip? The animators loaded up in a motor home and headed out for an adventure. As a result of their journey, you are able to see so many inspirations of the route in the movie. You can see a nod to the Wigwam Motel, the Cadillac Ranch, and the Tower Station and of course, Mater the truck was inspired by a truck spotted in Galena, KS. This movie did a beautiful job blending nostalgia with a message about the importance of community and the road less traveled.

Even the small screen got into action. The timeless TV series "Route 66," which graced screens from 1960 to 1964 with a whopping 116 episodes, solidified the highway's enduring presence in American pop culture. The show chronicled the journeys of two adventurous men traversing the road in their Corvette, providing a captivating lens into the multifaceted landscapes and narratives of America. However, what often goes unnoticed is the extraordinary behind-the-scenes challenges it faced. Filmed entirely on location, the production team often found themselves running out of scripts mid-season, leaving them in suspense. The crew lived on the edge, facing constant last-minute script revisions, cast changes, and even unexpected shooting alterations, creating an environment of unpredictability that made everyone's job remarkably challenging. Despite these obstacles, "Route 66" remains an iconic portrayal of American road culture. Along with the love of the classic Corvette.

Route 66 has always been a melting pot of cultures, which is reflected in its influence on the arts. The road runs through small towns and big cities, each contributing its unique flavor to the texture of American culture. This diversity is celebrated in the myriad of festivals, art shows, and cultural events that take place along the route. Here are just a few of the celebrations you will find across the country that celebrates "The Mother Road".

1. Every June there is a 10-day Texas Route 66 Festival in Amarillo, TX complete with music, dancing, and of course a cattle drive.

2. Septembers are known for Chicago's Route 66 Mother Road Festival with music, a classic car contest, and great food

3. Maplewood Route 66 Celebration happens in September in Maplewood, MO, and brags of a classic car show, great food, and live music.

For a complete and up-to-date list, visit Route 66 festivals and calendar of events in 2023 and 2024 listed by state and city (route66road-trip.com).

4

Chapter 4

The Journey Today

The Route 66 of today is a mosaic of the past and the present, a road that still whispers tales of yesteryear while embracing the changes of a modern world. This chapter takes you on a journey along the contemporary Route 66, exploring how this historic road has adapted to the new millennium and what it offers to today's travelers.

Present-day Route 66 winds its way through dynamic urban centers, quaint rural communities, and tranquil natural vistas, providing a rich texture of experiences for those who embark on its journey. Although certain segments of the original highway have been replaced or have succumbed to neglect, the essence of Route 66 endures, safeguarded by the dedicated communities that dot its route and the passionate enthusiasts committed to upholding its heritage. Numerous organizations are devoted to preserving not only the road itself but also the historic buildings and the cherished way of life that define Route 66.

Travelers on modern Route 66 can enjoy a blend of historical attractions and contemporary amenities. Museums and visitor centers along the way offer insights into the road's history, while annual events like car shows, music festivals, and cultural celebrations keep the spirit of the old Route 66 alive.

In this modern digital age, Route 66 has undergone a remarkable transformation, extending its reach and impact far beyond the asphalt. Online platforms, such as social media networks, dedicated blogs, and specialized apps, have breathed new life into the historic highway. With all things digital, there are blessings and curses. With the rise of the www.com world, millions of millennials and Gen Zs can now experience the wonders of this lifestyle without leaving their home, however, the goal would be to coax them out to live the wonder and beauty that is Route 66. These digital hubs have become treasure troves of information, catering to both seasoned travelers and budding enthusiasts alike. Whether you're planning a journey, seeking to share your own Route 66 tales, or simply looking to connect with fellow road trip aficionados, the online realm offers a plethora of resources Some of the more popular podcasts include:

1. Route 66: The Mother Road
2. Route 66: One For The Road
3. Podcast by Route 66

The appeal of Route 66 today lies in its ability to offer something unique in a homogenized world. It's a road that tells a story, inviting travelers to slow down and explore places with character and history. From the neon-lit streets of Tulsa to the quiet deserts of Arizona, Route 66 offers a journey through the heart of America. During the bustling travel season, countless visitors journey along Route 66's various stretches, each seeking their own slice of Americana — be it indulging in the famous 'Ugly Crust Pie' or capturing a moment with the iconic Blue

Whale of Catoosa, OK. No matter how familiar these attractions may be, it's the journey itself that keeps us, coming back. Its the open highway, the essence of exploration and timeless charm.

5

Chapter 5

Hidden Gems and Lesser-Known Facts

One lesser-known gem is located amidst the vast Arizona desert, the now-abandoned Painted Desert Trading Post stands as a poignant relic of a bygone era. It serves as a living testament to the once-thriving roadside commerce that was emblematic of Route 66's history, offering visitors a captivating glimpse into its commercial past and the stories it holds within its walls.

Another gem is a whimsical and intentionally tilted water tower, this quirky roadside attraction was a clever marketing tactic aimed at captivating the attention of passing travelers. To this day, it remains a distinctive and fun photo opportunity, reflecting the ingenuity and charm of Route 66's unique roadside attractions.

How about we look beneath the layers of Route 66 history where lies the lesser-known legend of the "Red Ghost." This enigmatic creature was said to haunt the deserts of Arizona during the late 19th century, adding an element of mystery and folklore to the landscape along the route.

Now we delve into the world of folk art and Native American heritage at Totem Pole Park, home to the world's largest concrete totem pole. Nestled in the heart of Oklahoma, this park serves as a hidden gem along Route 66, showcasing the creativity and cultural richness that define the road's diverse tapestry.

Finally, we stop in Cuba, Missouri, a town which wears its vibrant history on its walls, thanks to the Route 66 Mural City. Wander through this picturesque town, and you'll encounter a striking gallery of Americana, where colorful murals recount the town's history and celebrate the legendary highway. It's an open-air canvas that brings the past to life and adds an artistic dimension to your Route 66 journey.

Pete's
GARAGE
Conway

6

Chapter 6

The People of Route 66

Route 66 is more than just asphalt and attractions; inside it beats a heart and it's a living, breathing entity shaped by the people who travel it and those who call it home. This chapter introduces you to the diverse collection of personalities along Route 66, each contributing to the road's vibrant and enduring legacy.

The shopkeepers, diner proprietors, and motel managers serve as the dedicated guardians of Route 66's enduring legacy. They play a pivotal role in sustaining the vibrancy of this historic route, ensuring that it remains a lively and welcoming pathway for travelers seeking adventure and nostalgia. These individuals, who have committed their lives to the preservation of Route 66's unique spirit, provide essential havens where travelers can gather, forge new memories, and exchange tales of the road. Their dedication extends beyond mere commerce; they are the custodians of an American legend, from the eclectic diner owners to the stewards of charming, small-town museums. Their narratives stand as a powerful tribute to the road's tenacity and its timeless allure.

Artists and Craftsmen: Delve into the world of skilled artisans whose creativity is fueled by the rich tapestry of Route 66's history and the diverse cultures it encompasses. These craftsmen and artists are not just preserving age-old traditions; they are actively infusing them with contemporary relevance, crafting pieces that resonate with the soul of the Mother Road. Their work is not only a celebration of the past but also a vibrant, living part of Route 66's ongoing story.

Among the notable figures along Route 66, Bob "Crocodile" Lile stands out as a multifaceted personality. Not only does he serve as a knowledgeable Route 66 tour guide and historian, but he also showcases his artistic talents. As the proud owner of a shop situated right on Route 66, Bob offers a remarkable collection of meticulously crafted jewelry pieces. These unique creations are fashioned from paint taken directly from the iconic Cadillac Ranch, an emblematic Route 66 landmark. Through a meticulous and innovative process, Bob transforms this paint into exquisite jewelry, which he affectionately christens "Cadilite."

Paint Chip taken from a car

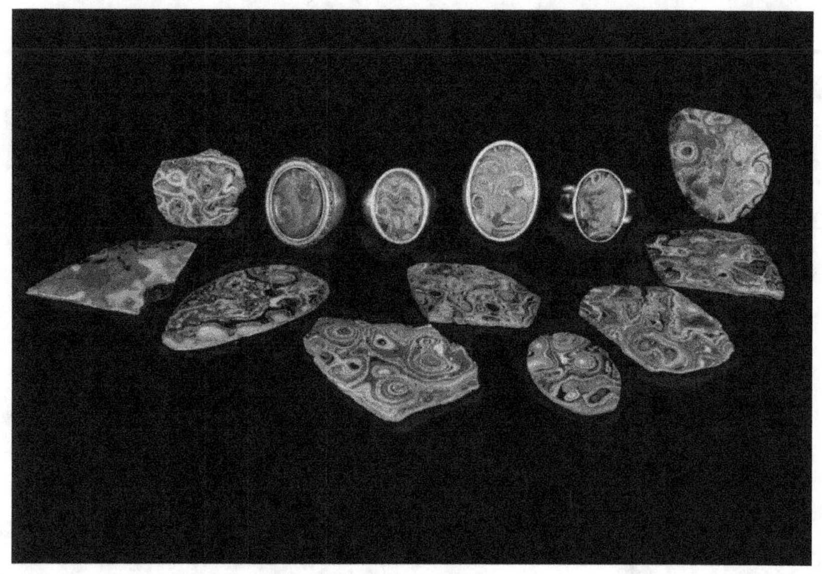

After the treatment by Bob

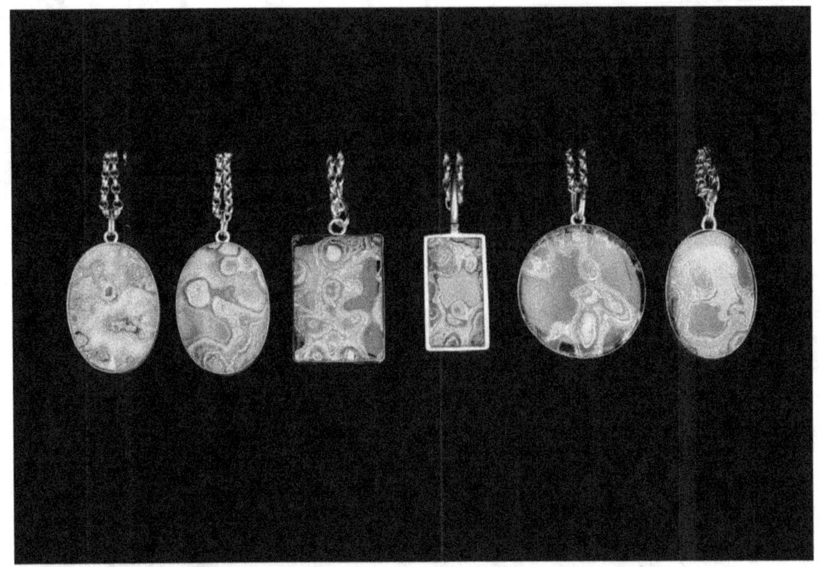

Every piece of Cadilite is a one of a kind

For those eager to explore Bob's artistic world, a visit to his charming shop, aptly named the "Lile Art Gallery," is an enriching experience. There, you can witness firsthand the captivating Cadilite jewelry collection, each piece bearing the essence of Route 66's storied past. Alternatively, enthusiasts can browse his collection online at Lile-gallery.com, where the legacy of this exceptional artist and his unique jewelry creations are accessible to a broader audience. Bob Lile's fusion of artistry, history, and the iconic Route 66 spirit is a testament to the boundless creativity and inspiration found along this legendary highway.

Nestled right in the heart of Route 66, you'll discover the charming town of Adrian, Texas, and its hidden gem, The Midpoint Cafe. This delightful diner is renowned for serving up the world-famous Ugly Crust Pies, a treat you won't want to miss. As you savor a slice of pie, you'll be regaled with the fascinating story of Fran Hauser, the cafe's former owner, who served as the inspiration for the beloved character Flo in the animated movie "Cars." Don't forget to explore the cafe's enticing gift shop, brimming with Route 66 memorabilia and souvenirs, making your visit an all-encompassing experience of nostalgia and hospitality.

The people of Route 66 are as diverse as the road itself, coming from all walks of life and every corner of the globe. Their stories reflect the changing face of America and the enduring appeal of the road. It's through their eyes that the true spirit of Route 66 is revealed – not just as a historic highway, but as a journey of discovery, connection, and renewal. All one needs to do is to look at the guest list of these locations and you will see the worldwide cultures that visits. I have asked one of the owners about his visitors and he told me that approximately 60% of his guests are from Europe. In fact, in the summer Route 66 is a huge European attraction. The big thing is to fly over rent a car and drive the road. A quick Google search will pull up many blogs sharing their stories of traveling, "The Mother Road" and giving others advice of the same. It is a bucket list item for many of our cousins across the pond. If you "ever plan to motor west' as the song goes and you run into those who are adventuring to do the same, please take the time to listen to their stories and share yours. It is time to create some beautiful memories.

Chapter 7

The Natural Landscape

Route 66 is far more than a mere conduit linking towns and cities; it represents a journey through some of the most varied and breathtaking landscapes America has to offer. In this chapter, we embark on a scenic exploration of the natural wonders dotting the Mother Road, illustrating how its geography profoundly shapes the experience of this iconic highway.

Our journey commences in the heartland, amidst the lush, rolling plains of Illinois and Missouri. This region, with its vast fields and expansive skies, instills a sense of boundless possibility that has long been synonymous with Route 66.

Transitioning into The Great Plains and Texas Panhandle, the road stretches into Oklahoma and Texas, where the landscape dramatically unfolds into the wide, windswept expanses of the Great Plains. Here, the horizon stretches to infinity, and the vast sky country captivates with its breathtaking sunsets.

As we progress, The High Desert of the Southwest beckons. Entering

New Mexico and Arizona, Route 66 cuts through the starkly beautiful high desert. Renowned for its mesas and rock formations that appear to glow red under the setting sun, this region is a testament to the road's diverse character.

Further along, we encounter The Painted Desert and Petrified Forest, natural marvels that provide a window into the earth's ancient history. Here, the colorful badlands and fossilized remains of forests, dating back millions of years, underscore the temporal depth of the journey.

Next we shift to The Mojave Desert, where the road ushers travelers into the mystical and arid landscape of sand dunes, Joshua trees, and rugged mountains – a realm that has long inspired artists and wanderers.

Our route culminates with The San Bernardino Mountains and the Pacific Coast, where Route 66 meanders through the verdant San Bernardino Mountains, ultimately leading to the Pacific Ocean. The journey reaches its zenith with the stunning coastal vistas of Santa Monica, marking a fitting end to this remarkable expedition.

We not only celebrate the beauty of these changing landscapes but also underscore the necessity of preserving them. As the popularity of Route 66 continues to soar, safeguarding its environmental heritage has become crucial, ensuring that this iconic route remains a testament to America's natural splendor for generations to come.

HISTORIC
ROUTE
66

8

Chapter 8

Culinary Journey

Route 66 is not just a feast for the eyes and the soul; it's also a journey of flavors and culinary traditions. This chapter takes you on a gastronomic tour along the Mother Road, exploring the diverse food culture that has grown and evolved with the highway.

Classic Diners: The quintessential Route 66 experience includes stops at vintage diners that have been serving travelers for decades. From the neon signs to the checkerboard floors, these diners offer a taste of nostalgia along with their menus.

Drive-Ins and Roadside Eateries: These establishments, often family-owned, provide a glimpse into the local flavors and specialties of the regions they inhabit. They're not just places to eat; they're part of the Route 66 community.

Regional Delights and Signature Dishes

Midwestern Comfort Food: In the heartland, comfort foods like meatloaf, fried chicken, and hearty pies dominate the menus, reflecting the agricultural roots of the region.

Southwestern Flavors: As the road progresses through Texas, New Mexico, and Arizona, the cuisine takes on a spicy, vibrant character with Mexican and Native American influences. Dishes like chili, enchiladas, and tamales are staples here.

California Fusion: The end of the road brings a fusion of flavors, with fresh seafood, Asian influences, and the health-conscious cuisine that California is known for.

The foods of Route 66 have evolved with the road itself. Once simple fare for travelers, the cuisine along the route now encompasses a wide range of styles and flavors, reflecting the diversity of the communities that line the highway.

Food on Route 66 does more than satisfy hunger; it tells stories. Each dish, whether it's a slice of pie from a small-town diner or a gourmet meal in a city restaurant, carries with it a piece of history and a connection to the people and places of Route 66.

Here are my top restaurants 5 for Route 66 (in no particular order)

1. Mid Point Cafe (Adrian, Tx)
2. The Big Texan (Amarillo, Tx)
3. Cozy Dog Drive-In (Springfield IL)
4.Big Vern's (Shamrock)
5. Waylan's Ku Ku Burger (Miami, OK)

Let's also looks at the future of dining along Route 66. With a growing interest in culinary tourism, many Route 66 eateries are finding new ways to attract and delight visitors, blending tradition with innovation. The website drivingroute66.com is a wealth of information for all things Route 66. I highly recommend it WHEN you are planning your vacation.

9

Chapter 9

Route 66 by the Numbers

Let's take a moment to delve into the fascinating world of Route 66 through a different lens: numbers. By exploring the statistics and figures associated with this iconic highway, we gain a unique perspective on its history, impact, and enduring legacy.

Spanning an impressive length of approximately 2,448 miles (3,940 kilometers), Route 66 offers a grand journey from the bustling streets of Chicago to the sun-kissed beaches of Santa Monica. This iconic highway weaves its way through a diverse array of American landscapes, crossing eight states: Illinois, Missouri, Kansas, Oklahoma, Texas, New Mexico, Arizona, and California. Along this expansive route, travelers experience a journey through time as well as space, passing through three distinct time zones, each adding its unique rhythm to the Route 66 experience. This remarkable expanse and the variety of regions it encompasses make Route 66 a quintessential representation of the American spirit of adventure and exploration.

For 59 years, from its official establishment in 1926 until its de-

35

commissioning in 1985, Route 66 stood as a main artery of American travel, weaving a rich tapestry of historical and cultural significance. Throughout its nearly six-decade-long tenure, this iconic highway carved a path through over 90 counties, stitching together a diverse cross-section of the American landscape. Along its winding route, Route 66 is dotted with hundreds of registered historic landmarks, each serving as a testament to the road's profound impact on American culture and history. These landmarks, ranging from classic diners and vintage motels to significant cultural sites, have collectively enshrined Route 66 not just as a road, but as an enduring symbol of America's evolving story, capturing the essence of the nation's spirit and heritage.

Route 66, officially established in 1926 and decommissioned in 1985, served as a pivotal main highway for 59 years, playing a crucial role in American transportation and cultural development. This historic route traversed over 90 counties, weaving through diverse landscapes and communities, each adding its unique character to the road's rich tapestry. Along its path lay hundreds of registered historic sites, each a piece of the intricate mosaic that makes up Route 66's cultural and historical legacy. Beyond its cultural impact, Route 66 was a significant economic artery, creating countless jobs and supporting local economies across its vast stretch. These jobs ranged from direct employment in diners, motels, and gas stations to indirect opportunities in tourism and related industries, underlining the road's role as a lifeline for many communities it passed through. This combination of historical significance, cultural richness, and economic impact cements Route 66's legacy as more than just a road, but a symbol of American growth and evolution.

Every year, Route 66 beckons millions of tourists from all corners of the globe, drawn irresistibly to its unique blend of history, cultural richness, and the allure of classic Americana. This storied highway, stretching across the heartland of America, is dotted with a myriad of popular attractions that have become pilgrimage sites for those seeking a taste of the legendary Route 66 experience. Landmarks like the Cadillac Ranch in Texas, an iconic public art installation featuring half-buried Cadillacs, the distinctive Wigwam Motel with its tepee-shaped accommodations, and the renowned Santa Monica Pier at the route's western end, each attract hundreds of thousands of visitors annually. These attractions serve not just as reminders of the route's storied past, but as vibrant, active locations that continue to enchant and engage travelers in the enduring mystique of Route 66.

Despite the inevitable changes and rerouting over the years, a substantial portion of the original Route 66 still exists today, a testament to the dedicated preservation efforts that have been put forth to maintain this iconic piece of American history. These efforts have been bolstered by substantial funding, with millions of dollars invested into preserving and restoring Route 66. This financial support comes from a combination of public and private initiatives, reflecting a widespread recognition of the road's cultural and historical significance. These investments ensure that the legacy of Route 66 continues to be accessible and tangible, allowing future generations to experience a piece of America's storied past and preserving the road not just as a memory, but as a living, breathing route that continues to captivate and inspire.

No matter what the future holds, Route 66 still plans to be there. The community of business owners and travelers alike still hold to this belief that freedom and adventure await us on the open highway. The road was called the "Mother Road" for a reason. She continues to call us. In this post-lockdown, COVID world where so many are dealing with overwork, overload, overthinking over over over…we are all OVER it all. I think we need to get away. The " Mother Road" says it's time to unplug and get back to our roots, and to remember where we came from.

So here is a message to all my friends who may be looking for me.

In the words of some great philosophers…

-"Life is a highway"
-"Get your kicks…" well, you know the rest.

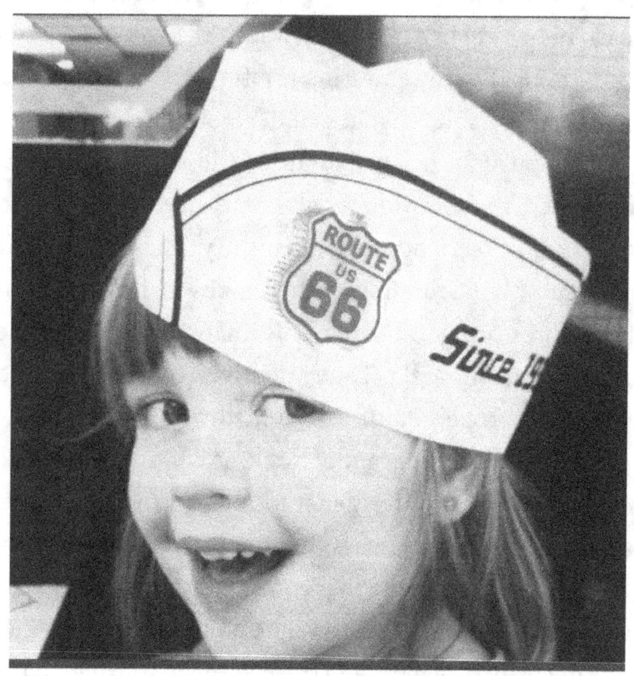

10

Conclusion

Conclusion: The Enduring Journey of Route 66

As we reach the end of our exploration of Route 66, it's clear that this iconic highway is much more than a stretch of pavement; it's a living testimony of American history, culture, and adventure. From its birth in the early 20th century to its enduring presence in the digital age, Route 66 has captured the imagination and hearts of millions, symbolizing a journey not just across landscapes, but through time itself.

The road's resilience, evidenced by the preservation of its landmarks and the revival of its spirit, speaks volumes about its significance. The collective efforts to maintain and celebrate Route 66, through both preservation and annual cultural events, ensure that its legacy continues to thrive. Its transformation from a major transportation route to a cherished historical artifact shows the road's adaptability and enduring appeal.

Moreover, Route 66's journey into the digital world has opened new avenues for its appreciation and exploration. The road's vast digital footprint, including websites, online communities, and social media platforms, has given it a new life, connecting enthusiasts from all corners of the globe.

As we close the cover to this book, it's evident that Route 66 is not just a road; it's a journey into the heart of America. It's a route that tells a story of change, resilience, and enduring charm. As travelers continue to traverse its path, whether physically or virtually, the spirit of Route 66 lives on, inviting us all to explore its history, experience its culture, and become part of its ongoing story.

In this book, "Route 66 Unplugged: Trivia, Fun, Food, and History…," we've journeyed through the past, present, and future of this legendary highway. The road ahead for Route 66 is as open and inviting as it has always been, beckoning new generations to discover its wonders and keep the spirit of the Mother Road alive for years to come.

Resources

Bellamy, S. (2022, June 25). *Highly recommended places to eat on Route 66 - Part 1.* Driving Route 66. https://www.drivingroute66.com/10-great-places-to-eat-on-route-66-part-1/

Bolstad, E. (2023, June 2). *Route 66, America's 'Mother Road,' readies for its centennial.* Missouri Independent. https://major-smolinski.com/NAMES/GETKICKS.html

https://missouriindependent.com/2023/06/02/route-66-americas-mother-road-readies-for-its-centennial/

Disney Pixar's Cars movie on Route 66 | ROUTE Magazine. (n.d.). https://www.routemagazine.us/stories/the-cars-story

Jain, S. (2023, September 17). Top 23 Route 66 attractions worth a stop - Santa Rosa Blue Hole. *Santa Rosa Blue Hole.* https://www.santarosabluehole.com/top-route-66-attractions-worth-stop/

Must Watch Movies filmed on Route 66 | ROUTE Magazine. (n.d.). https://www.routemagazine.us/stories/11-must-watch-movies

Route 66 Festivals and events. (n.d.). https://www.route66roadtrip.com/route-66-festivals-events-2023-2024.htm

Route 66: Perhaps TV's most labor-intensive show. (n.d.).